GHOST

Nick Conroy

Phil,

Love SWALC, love your stuff &
hope you enjoy the book.
Next Slam is yours!

Nick Conroy

Ghosts © 2019 by Nick Conroy.
Chief Editor: Wendy Pratt
Publishing Editor: Tracey Scott-Townsend
Cover Design by Tracey Scott-Townsend
ISBN: 978-1-9164896-1-5

English language edition published by Wild Pressed Books: 2019
Wild Pressed Books, UK Business Reg. No. 09550738
http://www.wildpressedbooks.com

Nick Conroy

Nick Conroy is a student at the University of Hull. He studied Philosophy with Creative Writing and is now starting a Master's degree in English, with a focus on Creative Writing.

Nick, who is originally from Kent, has been a Hull resident for around five years. *"It's here in Hull that my poetry has moved on leaps-and-bounds, and I continue to shape my style, and my voice, with influences I've been introduced to in this City."*

Nick loves performance poetry and has also been involved with the Contains Strong Language festival for the last two years, performing some pieces for BBC Humberside.

This is his first published collection of poems.

For Mum, for Granddad – my only ghost, for Dad, for Lauren, and for me.

Contents

Ghost 1

Wrong Morning 2

Love in the Cold 4

Shattered 7

The Bridge and the Quarry 8

Help or Spice 10

Dragonfly 12

Woes of One-Room Living 15

Stagnant 19

Solitude 20

Have you ever seen a ghost? 21

Grappling with Ghosts 24

For Mum 26

Grenade Fishing 27

Sisyphus 29

Buried Alive 31

Old Nail in a New Build 33

Paged Poetry 34

Sunken on the South Bank 36

Ghost

They say the house is haunted since we've been away,
and I can see the signs too, like traces of another life
that rubs itself across our paths, and breaks the midday haze.
A whisper unexpectedly announces through the too-bright-
for-background voice of the BBC presenter: "I'm off to bed",
and then silence for some longer. We share scared glances,
pretend it didn't happen and switch to Channel 4 instead.
Mugs of tea, too-milky and tepid, appear by chance,
with chewed on toast I swear I chucked that morning.
Some cigs still burn, breath on windows and when I turn,
I'm caught between his yawning from the room behind,
the open bottle of whiskey, and his pillbox on the side. One
day I'll catch the old man off-guard, pull him out of his trials
and sit him down with a pint, tell him it's been a while.

Wrong Morning

"Woke up on the wrong side of my head!"
I'd say, and everyone would have a good chuckle.

Well today I woke up blind,
and bleated for the stamps of sunfire
that jived trite in my peripheries.

"I've got train vision - no, TUNNEL vision!"
and they're all rolling on the floor.

I'll just spit out a prayer
for any commuter still on board.
Nothing worse than ash in your thoughts,
someone told me. Rodney, probably.
He's still mumbling over rosaries
on my chest of drawers.

"Eenie-meenie Del Boy!"
Everyone would have a good chuckle.

Meanwhile I'm obsessed
by the lip-red bricks
which make up my bedroom wall.
Derelict. Languid.
And their breath will always be
as angry as that which shapes the gaps
between each stutter of the wind between us.

2

This air is cursed to vex. Like me,
it hangs tempered for the tension
of each day it's left unbroken
by the passing tremor of an
honest body.

> *"There were two in the bed, and the little one left!"*
> *That was a good one, someone told me once,*

but I didn't know what they were trying to say.
I didn't know much back then, in truth,
but I knew more than I do now, and for that
I carve epitaphs into my memory walls,
caption each with promises,
promises I'll never keep, like:

> *"I'll be back."*

Everyone who's ever smiled to my eyes
rolls away like gunfire. Tonight,
I'll be forced to mine my empty ores,
tape down my curtain borders,
and chisel the sun out from my light.

Love in the Cold

One day, she sounded like
thick spits of rain
over drains filled with winter leaves
all squashed into coffee mulch.
That was spring, so I wondered if it had
planted something in my arteries.

The funny thing about spring
is the wait for something victorious,
like warm shadows, and two-pound t-shirts
replacing wish-I-could-buy-a-scarf Wednesdays.
Our skin was raincoat thin over
rattling timber bones,
like an empty bed frame;
shiver stiffened.

You see, back then, my only jacket
was breached battlements, split at seams
that I didn't even know existed,
while her parka was feline fur
wrapping matted spores like warm moss
around her neck. Yet still,
I've never tried so hard
to rid the cold from someone in all my life
with little more than
leftovers.

The heating in our flat had broken.
We didn't leave the bed
for longer than five unfed minutes.
When dusk had slipped the sun
from under us, we wandered dazed
in doubled-up clothes
for as long as our blue toes would let us.
Have you ever used a hairdryer
under your duvet for warmth?
Even my teeth were cold.

That was all of January,
and yawning through the month's frosty mornings
like cupping pale tea light cinders for palm warming
left big expectations
on February's
winter shoulders.

One day, she sounded like
the slow-creep of ice
over a kick-coughing car battery
we'd saved a quarter-grand to fix;
like pastille-melted walls
freezing into every single shade of
I'm done with this beige;
like oven gas through an open door
to try to cook the kitchen raw.
By March, the ice snapped off
and twisted itself into water,
and when April got tarpaulin with our last fiver,
we knew we couldn't wait for summer.

One day, in May,
she was my deepest breath,
and she sounded like afternoon maple.
I was the sound of tartan spotted damp
and some hour old gristle
before I could even catch up.

I can never hold onto this.
And when January beckons again,
with its same old nothing-to-do,
we know that we'll frighten ourselves recluse.

Shattered

Handcut glass, the box assures,
and already half shattered:
plastic chandelier smothered by whiskey rust.
Halfway to broken; even closer to weapon –
or as close as I was.

These morning bird hymnals
signal me away from night,
when some twist of ugly might encourage me
to dig the no-dirt from my nails;
to plant a scab over my knuckles;
to loose the freckles from my palm

Handcut. Handcut. Handcut.

The Bridge and the Quarry

The belly of the bridge sparked at midnight,
and by morning, no one could tell
how the fire had started.

Dust on duvets had lingered for too long
with full-stop belongings: sheet-fitted mattress,
desk lamp, curtain rails, PlayStation games,
a framed photograph which the coroner said
may have contained the remains of a
family dog.

It was early month and too early morning
for anyone to guess what else had survived the night.

That day, I cracked my foot-arch at school
(stupid kid, kicked a car). The hospital
plastered it up part-mummy,
and that stiff-leg tusk bore blushed cheeks from me
more than the hurt of it all.

A memorial of smoke, like moths,
balled up over the other arch, ceremoniously.
We couldn't *stand* that stench.
It busied itself from the bridge
to our front door for days and days
until the eyesore forced us tearful.

Back before, when he was a quarryman,
Granddad discovered the resting place of a Neolithic child.
Scurrying away wet clay from that girl's grave,
he soldered his fingers to the ground he departed,
and picked blue-grey grit from nailbeds
for all his days remaining.

He said they treated it like art,
and he cried a fortnight long that any child
should be carried from case to case.
Even so, they put the girl's bones in a
cold museum.

The bridge choked back its own child's dreams,
deep corbel sleep, easy on feet wrapped in blue
quarry clay and never mended the same.

Something in me learned that day
that graves can be bathed,
and will reach the museum case.
Other cases will stay closed in quiet.

Help or Spice

Have you ever been made to bear
the haunting of drum'n'bass, all fe-fi-fo-fum,
from a nearby club while you try to sleep?

In this lonely street, he could imagine
those bludgeon-elephant synths freeing him –
the pounding of impossible sound winding
round the handle on the side of his skull
'til his brain went jack-in-the-box
behind his footsteps.

That feeling floored him once,
in front of children, watching in silent fright
his thinness teeter, and drop nose-first
to knock concrete. They wouldn't understand
that symptom until memory of
him had already evaporated.

He became saturated with ground
as soon as he fell through it,
blended into the beehive cobbles that bedded
a dozen of him on all corners of this city –
a city that will forget his shadow's stain
on her doorsteps.

His head is an empty pillow;
he pulled the feathers out
when he was sleeping so that he could dream of a way
to mend the soggy tea-bags snagged
under his eyes.

His smile is a lie. His reality is spiked,
and every syllable he salivates through
is spelling either "help" or "spice".
Help or spice. What a choice when the cold
is costing layers of life for every blue fingertip
he tries to ignore.

He imbibes the moss on this floor he's heir to.
He survives solely so we can gloss him out from
council-costed quainteries, and he's there
through every wet-frost afternoon that we all decided
to stay at home through.

He leaves the smell of rot
from two-toke-choke bedlam no-bone zoots,
and every time we turn and twist a stern
tooth to him, he needs a full kingskin
tourniquet, because at least *that* owes him
some respite.

Have you ever swayed to someone else's drum'n'bass
when you're standing all alone outside? He lights,
he loses his mind, and those mammoth-monster synths
tug his chest from under him.

Tomorrow, we'll find him paralysed, only just alive,
until the police find a reason to
indict him.

Dragonfly

Now she wears a dragonfly necklace wherever she goes.
When those sapphire eyes blink at her from her chest,
she clasps her shoulders back and glides with a lion-taming strut,
like it might cut loose for a comfier nest at any sharp jolt.

I know this cycle. I've been warned of this revolt
in a bedtime long ago, when she told me that
dragonflies were dragons once.
But centuries transformed them, they stole colour
from their shrinking wings
and turned them all-tail.

Dragons were about *belly-fire* and *fights.*
Their lives were all damsels and armoured knights,
tight skin and barley-malt sting, disco lights and a
thousand years to fly in. They could afford to
rack up mileage, these anchorless beasts.
With a stride bigger than their eyes they saw
Deli, Komodo, Tuscan castles with Dom Perignon
enough to escape this cider belch,
sticky hands fumbling through a Friday fiasco,
all for a brain-wobbling sobbing-yourself-sodden
kind of headache to grease the morning.
Dragons are grace making calamities of structure.

But you need a bit of structure, she used to say
writing down summer holiday jobs on a post-it
bound for my bedside, next to socks folded invariably
into rose bulbs of black-and-white.
I never cottoned on. But time agrees.
And so the dragons lost their dreams.

They stopped hitching breezes aimlessly,
found space in their days for dial-tones, invoices,
lukewarm cups of tea, all to replace the
dancing, bop-fun savagery of night.
The boredom of these years enclosed them
full-chrysalis, melted them down inside
boiler-burnt living room promises.
Metamorphosis, years and years of it,
wondering what on earth they've become.
Until, one day, suddenly, they'd

Huff! Shuffle off and jump out to stretch new
colour-catching window wings and break a new
canter – a buzz strut. Now, they're dragonflies.
They're able to find the zen in
pond-skimming through mosquito mist;
tense-hovering over prosecco picnics;
skinny-dipping in river dimples,
to treading toes at cliff-fist.

They close the door to morning orchestrations,
to packed lunches and pyjama school runs.
High chairs and funfairs hit a bonfire
back in the Neverland treehouse, they caught a whiff
and went up, like the beachfront summer
we never forget about.

And forget about the paddling pool barbecues,
the grazed knee kisses and grass stained
articles of school uniform; trouser seams
plucked away to make room for growing pains
and it pains her knowing that
she's seen the end of these days.

But she drives a new purpose now.
I've seen a glimpse, when she's fixing her face
and her eyes cross to zone in on her little wings.
She catches their sparkled wink in her teeth,
her grin, and she sticks her tongue out at the
woman in the wall, swipes her off, peels her
hair-to-knee from the mirror
with a shiver and a spin.

I still feel young, she'd say to me
so I'm young really. She tucks away scars
from sun she picked up in Greece, from bruises
and splinters that tempered her in another body,
another life that pesters her through memory
every time she dreams of flame.

So she dares to pray, *Dragonfly, Dragonfly*,
And she finds herself taking flight again.

Woes of One-Room Living

You wake up.
There's no need to get up,
you're already there.
Here is the only place you're going to go today.
Bleary blink an hour away and listlessly
stray to the sink for a piss –
as listless as you can be in a home
as small as this. Twelve feet by six,
and half the space is filled with clutter-minded stuff
the raw stink of it enough to make you feel drunk,
in this simple rough patch, this 'caved-in stint' –

don't-think-about-it don't-think-about-it.

Get a drink and splash your cheeks.
Rub toothpaste on your teeth as a little treat.
Get back on the bed but
don't go back under the sheets –
the sun is still shining after all.
Stare at the wall for 40 minutes.
Ignore the call that threatens your mood.
Pretend you're busy, like a normal human,
probably getting some food on your break
or in a meeting or with some mates
because that's what people wrestle with
when they're not sad-angry wrangling
some tangents in the thousands –

don't-think-about-it don't-think-about-it.

You're proud the sun's going down already.
The bed feels suitable, your head feels steady,
and you feel ready to make your evening into something,
help to make you feel accomplished, so
you crack open the laptop,
and you let the white, bright light
and warm fan wind melt you
and subdue you.
The dull horizon hue
slaps a xenon wash all
over you, and you can
set your mind on snooze
while you find your zen
in the desktop blue.
It's a beautiful illusion:
network inclusion that still excludes you.
Connected to a means of distraction
from the truth, and you tunnel-chisel your view
with the world removed and settle into...
a movie.
No surprises,
just one you've seen before,
something with a touch of the
forlorn, an edge of drama,
but not real enough to make you mourn
and make you bawl in some melancholic sojourn
and rally more honesty than you'd care to afford,
lose all allure from buzzing screens and stuffing your
thoughts -

don't-think-about-it don't-think-about-it
don't-think-about-it-anymore.

Your brain's becoming more deliciously blank.
You claw away from the brink,
you try to muster a wank,
and your hand already stinks from yesterday's plans,
but you bury those sentiments,
and you flirt a flank to spark your pants
and tempt your body with a brief odyssey
to crank one out – you hit play,
have a frank enterprise, you hit pause
and put the porn away. But the same thought
as always enters the fray and makes the case
that this is the only exercise you'll get today –

> *don't-think-about-it don't-think-about-it*

But you've thought about it now:
that sink-pit guilt and toxic-fume doubt
tussle deep in your belly, in your grumble-bowels
and your thin skin wants to shout but you
haven't even the motivation to open up your mouth.
You've barely spoken in a month you've barely even been out
and this room is ever shrinking it's not permitting thinking
you're sure you're never really getting out.
You're a prisoner to your apathy.
The word 'pathetic' has too much clout not to bound around
your skull like a klaxon getting louder and louder
til you're forced to stagger-walk –

> *calm your heaving-barely breathing*

– to the window, and make a jagged fall –

> *who could be outside – don't dare to look them in the eye*

but if you stick your snout out and in-deep the air
'til you're hoovering up half the atmosphere...

Then you will relax.
You will relax.
You will hear every axle and joint inside you
slide down from tiptoes and curl-cosy
in their brackets. You'll smell
the breath of the birds, and the grass,
you'll let go of your panic,
and the distant wheeze of cars
will coo you into calm,
into simple, pleasing static.

See, one-room-living isn't always easy,
nor is it fantastic. But it's your only real option
when all the monsters from your attic
can't compare to the shit-gut scare
of social ineptitude and its
frantic-inducing cycles of over-thought
and over-manic overtures that crescendo
over your whole planet.
The risk is just too great right now,
and you know you've almost had it
but one-room living is just kind of easy,
it's comfortable, it's habit
and to crack it you'll need more than
ham-handed promises and an attempt to make a stab at it
you can't just take a stand and try to salvage it
without understanding how you'll manage it.

Don't think about it, don't think about it,
don't think about it today.
Put the rational thoughts away.
One-room living isn't always easy,
but it's comfortable,
so for now, you'll stay.

Stagnant

Tar like wet sugar pools the spaces
        between my thinking,
and any second now one of these bubbles
          will burst.
This is s t a g n a n t.
        I s t a g n a t e.
I broil and brew all the colour from my
        conjurings, then
I leave them be. A thumb-covered flash,
disowned.
          Not me.

But stagnant isn't dead.

Moss-green slick and gravy-thick
afterthought of water,
who'd have figured that
this is life?

It screams beneath the surface –
    under that petri dish milkskin everything
      is cooking. It sizzles, it rises, it changes –
      it *lives.*
        And under this glaze,
            so will I.

Solitude

It's an enigma. Not a nearly-thing,
like sleep is a nearly-thing, or thought.
More like the breath of ice, the muscles
in each arching appendage of flame.
It's a fitting description, solitude, for
something not really there, just a
feeling of affairs; a meaningless
bargain with a broken lighter –
flint-struck, off-cogged, caged,
and your cigarette trembles between lips,
waiting patiently for a non-negotiable spark,
waiting to be inspired into something delicious,
something poisonous,
like solitude.

Have you ever seen a ghost?

You want to see a ghost?
I can tell you all about ghosts, my friend,
and I can help you get there too.
Doesn't take much more than a bit of nerve,
of which I'm sure
you're not shy.

You have to do exactly what I say.

Not a question, not a word,
I have your tongue, so not a sound.
I have your feet, I have your hands,
I have your lungs, right here,
so you don't do a thing
I haven't told you to.
Okay?

Run a bath. Instructions are clear –
do it fast. Make it cold,
real creep under your nail-beds-cold.
While it fills, go to a window.

It has to be a tall window,
with a clear view of the sky.
Find a cloud – there's always one –
the hermit cloud,
hidden between folds in those miles of empty.
Find it. Hold its gaze, and
Don't. Fucking. Blink.

Watch it disintegrate.

The bath should be done.

There is no requirement that you undress,
though I do find it's best,
as they can see right through you
and they hate shame.
All the same it should work anyway.

Get down on your knees, right at the edge.
Hold your wrists.
Feel the channels glug, the ropes
in constant shudder. Alive.

Place your palms flat on the bottom of the bath.

Don't be alarmed. Take a breath,
like it's your last,
then lower your head into the bath.

Again –
Hold it.
Hold. It.
Blood will beat your skull.
your chest will clutch in tight,
then roll and writhe, batter your ribs,
but they *will* come. Hold it still, here they come.

There: the fading embers of life, the thoughts that
whimper into your dimming brain, the pleas,
the redemption, the threats, the moments of regret,
things you never thought you'd say – ghosts, one and all –
murmurs of the soon-to-be-dead, words we keep
tight lip-locked in our precious living heads,
ready to drown us before we ever get the chance.
These are the ghosts, my friend,
and they never let you forget.

Pull your head from the water.
Look at your veins. Watch them twitch.

Alive. Alive. Alive.

Grappling with Ghosts

I'd be lying if I said that I hadn't seen this coming.
Truth is, I caught a glimpse of the meat of your ghost
years ago. Eleven pints deep, and in a heaven
full of smoke, your eyes looked like they were
melting off the end of your nose.

You looked ready to drop. I'm sorry.
You looked like hell. I'm sorry.
I'm sorry, but just be straight and tell me –
did the fear of death leave you?

Did it stay in Spain,
when you woke up hot'n'cold and realised
the pain in your arm wasn't from that dodgy curry
the night before?

Did it flee from you in the hospital?
Your heart dribbling, slow-simmer,
after spilling over, you're hearing words
like *weeks, pneumonia.*
Did you grapple with your ghost?
Did you rehearse your punchline
so that any flatline can't take the last word?

Are you hearing me, Dad?
Did you think of me with the closure of a man
who's taking it all in while he knows he still can?
Did you say goodbye with enough sadness,
that when you survived you knew you couldn't
go back there, not while you still had
fight left in that mile-long patience
that you and I share?
I'm sorry.

I'm sorry because I know you care,
and I know you're scared,
and that the habits we kin perform
are often overbearing.

I have a feeling I'll be there one day,
caught out for shit decisions I've made
and feeling the close-to-chaos submission
that only comes in your final days.

It's unfair of me to expect more from you
than I'd ever expect from myself, isn't it?
You stopped being strong enough to lift monster trucks
and punch Godzilla into outer space
at the same time that I started to see my own errors
in the worry lines on your face.

I want to ask you to bring it back,
to pull off another impossible feat and
defeat any inkling of being beat before your time.
But your time isn't mine. Your time isn't mine.

And when I'm looking back on this,
with your same hair,
your same nose,
your same eyes,

I'll realise how much you tried,
and how you'll defy any odds
to spare another minute of your life
so that I'm spared a minute of crying.

But forever isn't real.
And you never even owned a monster truck.
I don't want to, dad, but I promise,
I am growing up.

For Mum

Nothing makes you as giddy as this.
Your three kids, round a table like
after-school dinner, only now we've
reconstructed the nest in our own styles
(each of them yours, each of them a slice of you).

No wine-high drunk can emulate this love,
and as you drag my neck to your chest and
squash me against you like you're printing braille
on my head, I know you're telling me something,
something I feel etched across my life.

And I know that if I reach up, twiddle
a vein of hair between my fingertips
and feel for the bumps at my roots,
I'll be able to spell out, with these abrasions
you cooked into me when I was nothing but
a firm kick deep in your gut:
"This is love, and it's always here."

Barcode braille.
I'm not always able to read it back to you,
but I can promise to scan it,
so your message will cut through all static
and brain-rain on pale days,
like sitting round the table after school,
like kicking your belly with
the faintest of knowing of who I will become,
but with every knowledge of who you are,
and certainty in my love for you.

Grenade Fishing

He dropped a grenade in a lake
in lieu of tackle and bait,
with the sentiment of skimming stones.

Isn't that cheating? is a stupid question
under a blister-sun like this.

The mountains, the mountains,
He smiled through lip tremors
and I knew not to laugh.
Can't you hear them?
We scouted silence, studious.

They listen, and they are danger.
But this doesn't sit right, because
danger means you hide.
No time for patience in fishing lines.
On these roads, no-noise brings them, angry.

I was a fresh-out-of-egg carp
with googly eyes: *but now they know*
where we are. Nothing dark as his
mile of stare and calibre laugh.

Yes, my boy, and they know we are armed.
A beetle hitches a ride on a skylark's toes
and I feel like any longer shade-less
will set me ablaze.

The fish float
               up,
and the boy sinks
                       low,
                             waiting for his own ride home.

Sisyphus

He seemed to me like a dirty bedsheet
draped over and pegged out during an
inconvenient storm.

His hands were inked gloves, cracked
with thick veins dripping from the topography
of his rubber-coarse skin.
Signs of water were surely
once found on him, but his moisture
had long ago evaporated.

His head was held intact
by a tightly-wound hard hat,
and I knew if you removed the straps
their shape would be stamped
like a footprint in snow
into his soot-soaked crown.

His cheeks had sunken into a
permanent frown, bulldog brows
overflowed his eyes to shield from the
shine of his twisted, torn hi-vis.

He didn't know it
but I saw the boulder on his back,
knew it was heavier than mine.
Knew that pain splashed over his face
was caused by scuffed out pencil scars
smudged there by a higher cause

and I knew that he'd carry that weight
like a soldier holding an enemy's gun
like a mother holding someone else's child,
like his thumbs on full wage before rent is paid.

Roll it, roll it all the way to the top.
Let it teeter, let it drop, and only on
the walk back down can you stop
and admire the world from a perch;
taste the clouds, smell the curve
of the earth, let sunset stain your eyelids
and help you to do it all again.

Buried Alive

I wonder how I'm going to bury you.
Like hitting a pillow hoping to reach the other side.
Tangled in the bog of sweat on sheets,
I'll stick out my feet through the neck of the beast
for the feeling of the breeze as it breathes me down.

I wonder how I'm going to bury you.
And what words will be sheathed in the treaty of peace?
In aid of mourning teas, toast never to be touched,
or the nonchalant chatter from distant TVs
sat idle in the other room, like Great-Aunt Louise
pestering your short hairs, never asked to leave.

I wonder how I'm going to bury you.
And which *you* will be the you that I forget last?
The unerring high-shoulder, slicker-than-a-Benz
friend to everyone, with hands I'd never grow into,
stories I'd never tire from, faint sandstone
stubble and strong knees for somersaults,
a kiss to carry me through sleep to morning.

I wonder how I'm going to bury you.
While you slumber on your arm at the bar,
A whole world away from any mumble
of my bumbling, desperate scrambling.
I notice you stare into the overhead lamp,
like it could burn you out before it blinds you.
So I pull out my phone, but I guess you see a shovel.

I wonder how I'm going to bury you.
Because as offensive as it seems, I'm grooming
back the hair you've now forgotten, for a casket fit,
and I'm sizing you up in your new shuffle-out frame,
thinner, and no doubt it'll change before I
lay a wreath on your chest or place a coin on your head,
and tell you that I've always loved you, again.

Old Nail in a New Build

The hammer that struck its head and plugged it
stopped beating iron long ago.
There must have been a purpose for this
rusty old puncturer. Crooked, proud, stamped
hard graft through brick and bone,
in a blind-handed effort at structure.

Maybe it was meant to pierce timber,
meant to hold the cross-eyed beams of its home –
it saw a nobler life in its flathead,
this relic of craft, now drowned in the flawless
dimensions of smooth, machine-wombed bricks
and impossible pillars of factory steamed steel;
stainless, no scars of age on this metal,
while the hand-loved iron of that four hundred
year-old's fettle is buried in the labyrinths
of refurbishments and do-overs. So it sits
unnoticed, unfazed, aware of its growing age.

But it still clings tight to its fittings,
finds some meaning in its strength,
knows that when some job's-worth lays his teeth
around its head, tries to tug it from its depth,
it'll go into the light kicking and screaming,
and the house will come falling next.

Paged Poetry

I can't write poetry in a notebook.
Binder paper rips are no replacement
for move-to-trash. Cross-outs are
useless anger, when you can still squint
letters under scrawls. But backspace
kills off a word
dead.

I don't even want a ghost of these metaphors.
They linger long enough, birthed through tooth gaps
and screaming from the first – thirsty crabs in a net
with not a pinch to pay their way
out of this mess.

Or the clothes you pass from wardrobe to charity shop,
their ambergris musk still patterns the sewings
you thought you looked good in,
and you'll never wash the loose of your
body from their stretch.

Don't you dare jump to brain-front.
I'm trying to forget you already.
I've pushed you onto ferries to tip out in
some distant ocean of my memory.

Because sometimes you're just forgettable,
untenable for me to put my weight onto.
I piggybacked you for one drink's worth
but I'm not waking up with you
tangled in my hair.
I wouldn't go there.

Not a nothing or a could be something –
some words just scrape the marrow
from your skull and ostentate you
blind lightning, like stomach tumbling sour
and too-sweet-to-bear gummies,
right molar stubborn verbs.

I can't write poetry in a notebook.
I'll just stick to the screen.
No one should be subject
to the secrets I'll unknowingly bleed,
so I'll just delete them with the data tide
and hope that they'll be deleted from me.

Sunken on the South Bank

I'm sunken and unspoken on the South Bank.
My phone's twice broken and only works on one side.
I've been drunk and alone since...
for a few months' time –
well, since the touchscreen was intact
and the front camera worked fine.

See, I smashed it pelting through Camden on a Boris Bike.
I'd cleared Soho with two pushes and in ten minutes
I was on the bridge at Waterloo, and I don't know if you've ever seen
the view, but the city was lit in this diamond-peppered hue,
with each office block chucking out different watts
of reds and greens and blues,
so that the tower-trodden horizon bragged more stylish lights
than the stars and moon,
and it made sense to me.

Because this is a city that's all about you,
and who you know, and what you can do,
but if you go there with your hands in your pockets
and your eyes at your shoes then it'll swallow you.
It'll chew you round its stone-tooth streets
and throttle you with endless adverts
for all that is decadent and fleeting.

But like any true Londoner the city averts its
sleepy eyes when you beg it for a little empathy:
a little vision to see past the disguise of hipster,
or gangster, or young professional,
or any other half-arsed alias –
See, half of these people are running
eight laps slow in their rat races.

The other half are running eight seconds slow,
and they're off their fat faces
so we don't look each other in the eye.
And we let the moments drag along
until they've finally passed us by.

So I was sunken – about ten seconds slower than the world –
when I crossed a lost gaze with this girl.
And with each step she left a current in the ground
that snaked out to my feet and set my chest rolling deep,
and I spotted sepia fingers of light that seemed to
stretch from the shine of her after-autumn auburn hair.
Her eyes lingered for just a fraction too long
on all the artefacts she set them on and I imagined her
philosophising, admiring with a keen mind
the cracked-kissed concrete and slapstuck bike lane lines.
I noticed her dodge the gaps in the slabs in her street
with a two-step jump routine, and with every jump
she was suspended at her trapeze peak...
and the city was suspended around her,
waiting for the punchline of her size five
New Balance sneakers landing safely on the other side.

I couldn't stand even if I'd thought to,
but there was no thought.
Her eyes found a bin, my bench, and then me.
but I didn't look away – I didn't drop my eyes
in embarrassment or shame, and for those swift seconds

the holes in my pockets were weightless,
and this cramped, lonely city deflated
so that the spaces between the boroughs
didn't seem so vacant and distrusting
but boundless and accustoming and filled with
excitement for the future, instead of fear.

I'm scared of being here.
I'm scared of the cogs and gears that grumble under the
pavement,
steer all these clockwork agents to their daily arrangements,
somehow keep the lights bright and the sewers fragrant.
I'm scared of getting lost in the river, in the gutters,
like quicksand I'll fall through the ground
and when I need a hand to help me out
no one can offer me much, but *sorry I'm in a rush*,
they'll chuck a few coppers or the leftovers of lunch.

It's the same fear that's got me glued me to this bench,
brave enough to hold this girl's gaze,
but ultimately just holding up pretence
because in a city this big it's hard to keep your friends,
and it's easier to let the moment pass
than it is to grasp it in the end.

So I smile to her.
Just the usual commuter half-smile,
with your lips more pulled back straight than curled up your
face,
so you're almost apologising for treading on the toes of their
day.
I don't wait to see if she smiles back at me –
I've already lowered my head in the shame of defeat,
arriving at the sinking truth that this inquisitive comet
blazing briefly across my sky, and I,
will almost certainly never meet.

So I'm sunken and unspoken in the break of morning
on the mouth of this South Bank bench.
My phone's been twice broken, and I'll always be falling,
unsure if I'll make it out of this city again.

Acknowledgements

Thank you, first and foremost, to Tracey & Phil Scott-Townsend at Wild Pressed Books. I can never thank you enough for giving me this opportunity to share my words. Thank you for your appreciation, your time, your dedication, and your patience. You're doing wonderful work, and you inspire me to keep writing.

Thank you, Mum. You were once my only ear for this wordy stuff, and I know you'll never stop lending me your patience, attention and love.

Thank you, Granddad. You taught me to embrace my creativity, and taught me that poems, like sadness, don't need an audience to have meaning.

Thank you, Lauren, for your love, and for helping me up when I was down.

Thank you to anyone who has approached me after a performance and told me how my poems have impacted them. Please don't be afraid to tell me about your experiences, or your art – you inspire me when you do.

Lightning Source UK Ltd.
Milton Keynes UK
UKHW011146010319
338265UK00001B/51/P